MAKE BRIGHT THE ARROWS

Books by

EDNA ST. VINCENT MILLAY

The Lamp and the Bell
Second April
Three Plays
Renascence
A Few Figs from Thistles
The Harp Weaver
Aria da Capo
The King's Henchman
The Buck in the Snow
The Princess Marries the Page
Poems Selected for Young People
Fatal Interview
Wine from These Grapes
Conversation at Midnight
Huntsman, What Quarry?
Make Bright the Arrows

*

Harper & Brothers
Publishers

Make Bright the Arrows

....

1940 NOTEBOOK

....

EDNA ST. VINCENT MILLAY

HARPER & BROTHERS *Publishers*
New York *and* London
1940

"Make bright the arrows; gather the shields: the Lord hath raised up the spirit of the kings of the Medes."

—Jeremiah LI-ii

Make bright the arrows,
  Gather the shields:
Conquest narrows
  The peaceful fields.

Stock well the quiver
  With arrows bright:
The bowman feared
  Need never fight.

Make bright the arrows,
  O peaceful and wise!
Gather the shields
  Against surprise.

CONTENTS

V

Sonnets

I

TO THE MAID OF ORLEANS

JOAN, Joan, can you be
Tending sheep in Domrémy?
Have no voices spoken plain:
France has need of you again?—

You, so many years ago
Welcomed into Heaven, we know,
Maiden without spot or taint,
First as foundling, then as saint.

Or do faggot, stake and torch
In your memory roar and scorch
Till no sound of voice comes through
Saying France has need of you?

Joan, Joan, hearken still,
Hearken, child, against your will:
Saint thou art, but at the price
Of recurring sacrifice;

Martyred many times must be
Who would keep his country free.

MEMORY OF ENGLAND

October 1940

I AM glad, I think, my happy mother died
Before the German airplanes over the English country-
    side
Dropped bombs into the peaceful hamlets that we used to
    know—
Sturminster-Newton, and the road that used to run
Past bridge, past cows in meadow,
Warm in the sun,
Cool in the elm-tree's shadow,
To the thatched cottage roofs of Shillingstone;
Dropped bombs on Romsey Abbey, where the aging rec-
    ords show
(Or did a little while ago)
In faded ink and elegant fine hand
The name of a boy baby christened there
In 15— (I forget the year)
Later to sail away to this free land
And build in what is now named Massachusetts a new
    Romsey here.
(My ancestor,—I still can see the page,
Our sentimental journey, our quaint pilgrimage!)

Dorset and Hampshire were our home in England: the
    tall holly trees, the chestnuts that we found
Glossy within their shaggy burrs on the cold autumn
    ground
In the New Forest, new in the Norman's day, where we
    walked alone,
Easing at times our joyful weary backs
By shifting to a stump the weight of our small shoulder-
    packs,
Meeting no living creature all one lovely day
But trees and ferns and bracken and, directly in our way
Or grazing near at hand,
From time to time a herd of small wild ponies; well aware
Of imminent sunset—and we two alone long miles from
    anywhere.

All that we moved among, heath, bracken, hollies with
    round berries red
Bright for an English Christmas, beech and oak,
Chestnut, with its sweet mealy food
On the leaves thick about us in the autumn air
Plentiful, gleaming from its rough burrs everywhere—
All this was good,
And all had speech, and spoke,
And all the magic unfamiliar land
Was ours by distant heritage and ours by deep love close
    at hand.

[5]

How many miles we walked I now forget, dog-tired at
    night
Spying an inn's warm light
Through small-paned windows thrown,—
To Romsey, and then back to Shillingstone.

So gravely threatened now
That lovely village under the Barrow's brow,
Where peering from my window at dawn under the shelv-
    ing thatch
With cold bare feet and neck scratched by the straw
I saw the hounds go by;
So gravely threatened the kind people there,
She in her neat front flower plot,
He like as not
Up in the 'lotment hoeing,
Or coming home to his supper of beer and cheese,
Bread and shallots,
These thoughts . . .
And thoughts like these . . .
Make me content that she, not I,
Went first, went without knowing.

I FORGOT FOR A MOMENT

July 1940

I FORGOT for a moment France; I forgot England; I forgot
    my care:
I lived for a moment in a world where I was free to be
With the things and people that I love, and I was happy
    there.
I forgot for a moment Holland, I forgot my heavy care.

I lived for a moment in a world so lovely, so inept
At twisted words and crookèd deeds, it was as if I slept
    and dreamt.

It seemed that all was well with Holland—not a tank had
    crushed
The tulips there.
Mile after mile the level lowlands blossomed—yellow
    square, white square,
Scarlet strip and mauve strip bright beneath the brightly
    clouded sky, the round clouds and the gentle air.
Along the straight canals between striped fields of tulips
    in the morning sailed
Broad ships, their hulls by tulip-beds concealed, only the
    sails showing.

[7]

It seemed that all was well with England—the harsh foreign voice hysterically vowing,
Once more, to keep its word, at length was disbelieved, and hushed.

It seemed that all was well with France, with her straight roads
Lined with slender poplars, and the peasants on the skyline ploughing.

I DREAMT THE LOWLANDS

I DREAMT the Lowlands still were free.
That the big wind-mill and the pollard willow, the knot-
    willow tree,
Beside the still canal, that the knot-willow still was free.

Small Holland, that had held away
The sea
So many years; with three
Great man-made dykes, The Watcher, The Dreamer
    and The Sleeper, held away
The sea;
Poured into now, now inundated from the dykeless side,
By Germany,
More ruthless than the sea,
For the sea, though stern and cold, had never lied.

Drowned land, drowned land.
Poor Holland, decent men,
Great engineers,—had you no fourth dyke, then,
Dyke called The Spyer, dyke against treachery?

(Note: *A part of Holland, a stretch of coast-line on the North
Sea, is protected from inundation by three dykes, one behind the
other, known as "De Waker, de Droomer, en de Slaper". If the
Watcher (or Waker) which fronts the sea, should be broken, the
Dreamer would rouse; if the Dreamer were overcome, the Sleeper
would wake.*)

AN ECLIPSE OF THE SUN IS PREDICTED

I NEVER was one to go to war against the weather, against
    the bad conditions
Prevailing, though prevailing for a long time, the sullen
    spring,
The ugly summer grey and cold;
"Summer will bud"; I said; "Autumn do the blossoming;
Winter curtail a year without fruitions;
I, starving a little, await the new bounty as of old."

I have gone to war, I am at war, I am at grips
With that which threatens more than a cold summer;
I am at war with the shadow, at war with the sun's eclipse,
Total, and not for a minute, but for all my days.
Under that established twilight how could I raise
Beans and corn? I am at war with the black newcomer.

II

THERE ARE NO ISLANDS ANY MORE

May 1940
*(Lines Written in Passion and in Deep Concern for
England, France, and My Own Country)*

DEAR Isolationist, you are
So very, very insular!
Surely you do not take offense?—
The word's well used in such a sense.
'Tis you, not I, sir, who insist
You are an Isolationist.

And oh, how sweet a thing to be
Safe on an island, not at sea!
(Though someone said, some months ago—
I heard him, and he seemed to know;
Was it the German Chancellor?
"There *are* no islands any more.")

Dear Islander, I envy you:
I'm very fond of islands, too;
And few the pleasures I have known
Which equalled being left alone.
Yet matters from without intrude
At times upon my solitude:
A forest fire, a dog run mad,

[13]

A neighbour stripped of all he had
By swindlers, or the shrieking plea
For help, of stabbed Democracy.

Startled, I rise, run from the room,
Join the brigade of spade and broom;
Help to surround the sickened beast;
Hear the account of farmers fleeced
By dapper men, condole, and give
Something to help them hope and live;
Or, if Democracy's at stake,
Give more, give more than I can make;
And notice, with a rueful grin,
What was without, is now within.

(The tidal wave devours the shore:
There *are* no islands any more)

With sobbing breath, with blistered hands,
Men fight the forest fire in bands;
With kitchen broom, with branch of pine,
Beat at the blackened, treacherous line;
Before the veering wind fall back,
With eyebrows burnt and faces black;
While breasts in blackened streams perspire,
Watch how the wind runs with the fire
Like a broad banner up the hill—
And can no more . . . yet more must still.

[14]

New life!—to hear across the field
Voices of neighbours, forms concealed
By smoke, but loud the nearing shout:
"Hold on! We're coming! Here it's out!"

(The tidal wave devours the shore:
There *are* no islands any more)

This little life, from here to there—
Who lives it safely anywhere?
Not you, my insulated friend:
What calm composure will defend
Your rock, when tides you've never seen
Assault the sands of What-has-been,
And from your island's tallest tree,
You watch advance What-is-to-be?

(The tidal wave devours the shore:
There *are* no islands any more)

Sweet, sweet, to see the tide approach,
Assured that it cannot encroach
Upon the beach-peas, often wet
With spray, never uprooted yet.
The moon said—did she not speak true?—
"The waves will not awaken you.
At my command the waves retire.
Sleep, weary mind; dream, heart's desire."

[15]

And yet, there was a Danish king
Assured he governed everything.
He bade the ocean not to rise.
It did. And great was the surprise.

No man, no nation, is made free
By stating it intends to be.
Jostled and elbowed is the clown
Who thinks to walk alone in town.

We live upon a shrinking sphere—
Like it or not, our home is here;
Brave heart, uncompromising brain
Could make it seem like home again.

(There are no islands any more.
The tide that mounts our drowsy shore
Is boats and men,—there is no place
For waves in such a crowded space.)

Oh, let us give, before too late,
To those who hold our country's fate
Along with theirs—be sure of this—
In grimy hands, that will not miss
The target, if we stand beside
Loading the guns (resentment, pride,
Debts torn across with insolent word—
All this forgotten, or deferred
At least until there's time for strife

Concerning things less dear than Life;
Then let, if must be, in the brain
Resentment rankle once again,
Quibbling and Squabbling take the floor,
Cool Judgment go to sleep once more.)

On English soil, on French terrain,
Democracy's at grips again
With forces forged to stamp it out.
This time no quarter!—since no doubt.

Not France, not England's what's involved,
Not we,—there's something to be solved
Of grave concern to free men all:
Can Freedom stand?—Must Freedom fall?

(Meantime, the tide devours the shore:
There *are* no islands any more)

Oh, build, assemble, transport, give,
That England, France and we may live,
Before tonight, before too late,
To those who hold our country's fate
In desperate fingers, reaching out
For weapons we confer about,
All that we can, and more, and now!
Oh, God, let not the lovely brow
Of Freedom in the trampled mud

Grow cold! Have we no brains, no blood,
No enterprise—no any thing
Of which we proudly talk and sing,
Which we like men can bring to bear
For Freedom, and against Despair?

Lest French and British fighters, deep
In battle, needing guns and sleep,
For lack of aid be overthrown,
And we be left to fight alone.

BALLADE OF LOST CITIES

Where is the proud, the ancient town
Prosperous once, now sore distressed?—
Rotterdam, name of sad renown,
Antwerp and Brussels, Ghent and Brest,
Tamed or destroyed at whose behest?
Cherbourg, Ostend, le Havre, Calais,
Warsaw and Prague and Bucharest—
Where are the towns of yesterday?

Leyden, Louvain in her new gown,
Rheims and Rouen, and Lourdes the blest,
Vichy, in shameful shirt of brown,
Paris, of cities loveliest
Bitterly now in mourning dressed;
Deauville, Vienna once so gay,
Calvados, where the cider's best,—
Where are the towns of yesterday?

Obsolete now, though still a noun,
Honour can not disturb his rest,
Softly he sleeps on eider-down,
Dreaming, perhaps, of Budapest,
Athens and Istambul hard-pressed,
Cairo, Hong-kong, Peking, Cathay,
Singapore, Moscow—*there's* a jest!—
(And where are the towns of yesterday?)

Envoi
President, why the lack of zest?—
Washington's safe—who'd dare assay
Boston, New York, the Middle-West? . . .
But where are the towns of yesterday?

INTELLIGENCE TEST

Q: WHAT, if anything, would you do
To keep your country free? . . . *A:* Lay
Down my life! *Q: You?* You mean you'd *die?*
A: Certainly. (*Chorus:* That's a lie.)
Q: For your country's defense, how much would you
    give,—
If it weren't taxed out of you, I mean. *A:* All that I have.
Q: You?—You mean *money? A:* Certainly I do.
All that I have. (*Chorus:* Lie. You wouldn't give ten
    cents.)

Q: You, young man out of a job, but eating hearty
Still, somehow, at the State's (*L'Etat c'est moi's*) expense,
Would you join the army for a year—for the State's de-
    fense,
Just in case, you know—get up early, learn to handle a
    gun,
Drill, take orders? . . . *A:* I certainly would!
I'd join for two years, three, give up my babyhood!
(*Chorus:* That's a lie. At least, unless you thought it fun.)

_Q_: You, young woman out of finishing-school unfin-
  ished:
To preserve Free Speech, would you give up going to a
  party,
Going to the movies just once, one shopping-trip in
  town?—
I mean by "Free Speech" your right to call your father
  down
In front of his friends, for drinking Martinis, laughing too
  loud,
Trying to act young; for your right to tell his age before a
  crowd
Of girls who think him charming,—for your Uncivil Lib-
  erties undiminished,
For your right to rise late, to keep the radio roaring all day
When everybody else wants to read or rest, or has some-
  thing to say
Of interest to somebody else—for the American Way
Of Living—what would you pay? . . . _A:_
I see no reason why I should sacrifice myself; the Younger
  Generation
Sees no reason at all why it should sacrifice itself for a
  nation
In which the rich oppress the poor, where the plutocrat
  lolls in his limousine while the working-man walks:
I know all about it; I belong to a Movement; we've had
  lots of talks;

For a Capitalist Government which tramples on the
    Worker and his hungry children and wife,
The Younger Generation refuses to do anything at all!—
    I didn't ask to be born, did I?—We demand our
    right to a normal, healthy life!

OVERHEARD AT A BAR

A. BETTER think up your answers *now*,—and have them
    ready.
    Question's bound to come up.
    Supposing England *doesn't* win the war!—are you
      prepared to—

B.   Steady,
    Old boy. Is that a way to talk? Now, listen: that lov-
      ing-cup
    That Hitler's handing 'round to all those nations over
      there (not very thirsty, I guess,—ha! ha!—poor
      devils, scared stiff to make a fuss)
    That's no mint julep, my lad, that's *poisonous,*
    That's what it is, it's *hemlock,*—understand me?—
      and if England *didn't* win the war, why it might
      get 'round to *us!*

A. Well, why shouldn't I say, then, if England *doesn't*
    win—

B.   Good God, it's *blasphemous!*

C. That's right, my boy: *we* can't police two seas.

A. Just what I was *saying,* you sponge-head!

C.   All right, now. Please
    Keep that in mind. What you called me, I mean. Now
      suppose
    I resented your calling me a sponge-head—just sup-
      pose I did—

[24]

And somebody heard about it, and told my kid,—
My boy, fourteen—that I'd just better not get tough
With you, because I couldn't lick you, I wasn't big
    enough:
What would that do to my boy—to his self-esteem?—
Understand me?
A. Sure I understand you. You're living in a dream.
    That's easy enough to understand. You're living in a
    dream.
    And if England loses this war—
B.   But she *can't!* It's *impossible!* Don't you see,
    For God's sake, if England lost this war, where WE
    would be?

"AND THEN THERE WERE NONE"

Ten white ptarmigan
  Perching in a pine;
Hitler gave his solemn oath:
  And then there were nine.

Nine white ptarmigan
  Trusting in their fate;
Hitler gave his solemn oath:
  And then there were eight.

Eight white ptarmigan
  Putting trust in Heaven;
Hitler gave his solemn oath:
  And then there were seven.

Seven white ptarmigan
  In a pretty fix;
Hitler gave his solemn oath:
  And then there were six.

Six white ptarmigan
  Hoping to survive;
Hitler gave his solemn oath:
  And then there were five.

Five white ptarmigan
　Wishing they were more;
Hitler gave his solemn oath:
　And then there were four.

Four white ptarmigan
　Trying to agree;
Hitler gave his solemn oath:
　And then there were three.

Three white ptarmigan
　Feeling very few;
Hitler gave his solemn oath:
　And then there were two.

Two white ptarmigan
　Cried, "It can't be done!"
Hitler gave his solemn oath:
　And then there was one.

One white ptarmigan
　Looked about and blinked;
Hitler gave his solemn oath:
　The race is now extinct.

III

UNDERGROUND SYSTEM

(From *Huntsman, What Quarry?*)

SET the foot down with distrust upon the crust of the
    world—it is thin.
Moles are at work beneath us; they have tunnelled the
    sub-soil
With separate chambers; which at an appointed knock
Could be as one, could intersect and interlock. We walk
    on the skin
Of life. No toil
Of rake or hoe, no lime, no phosphate, no rotation of
    crops, no irrigation of the land,
Will coax the limp and flattened grain to stand
On that bad day, or feed to strength the nibbled roots of
    our nation.

Ease has demoralized us, nearly so; we know
Nothing of the rigours of winter: the house has a roof
    against—the car a top against—the snow.
All will be well, we say; it is a habit, like the rising of the
    sun,
For our country to prosper; who can prevail against us?
    No one.

The house has a roof; but the boards of its floor are rot-
    ting, and hall upon hall
The moles have built their palace beneath us: we have
    not far to fall.

THE BLIZZARD

ARE we not wise who wear in winter warmer clothing
Than when the summer days are hot?
Do you not utter folly who insist in winter when the day
    is cold, that it is not?

Forced out of doors in winter in a paper dress, holding the
    broom
Thrust into your hands, chattering and weeping, I have
    seen you go
Who have no choice, poor child, being under-fed, con-
    fused and frail;
I pity you; I hope you will find, as in the fairy-tale
Strawberries under the snow.

But for the nourished, the fit, the able to think and to act,
    the stout,
Who sit in winter by the fire in a pleasant room,
Curtains drawn,
Delicate sandal or varnished shoe by the comfortable blaze
Warmed, and gently glowing,
Talking of summer, planning for the summer days
To come, laughing above the menace of the wind, never
    looking out
To see that the snow is twelve feet deep on the lawn . . .
And still snowing . . .

Not brave, solemnly warned, waving aside the warning:
"This snow, if it keeps on, will be up to the eaves by
    morning!"
Under a weight too great this roof can fall,
This ceiling vomit snow like broken plaster upon all,
Submerging them, like a reversed volcano, in frigid
    snow—
And out of here nowhere to go—
The first man at the door heard sharply to shout,
"Jesus! For God's sake let me out!"—
Then stagger back like a corpse to its roomy grave
From what's outside—Behave
With courage or even taste, who will?—the gilded slipper
    in the tripped face
Will make its cut, erased
At once by the broader heel;
Women will scream and claw, men curse and crowd (no
    blame
For this from me, who well might—oh, I trust not!—do
    the same)
I deplore the idle scorning
Only, of the solemn warning.
Guests, host and hostess unprepared:
Everybody warned; nobody scared.
And not so much from unbelief or courage, this,
As indolence and listlessness.
Who wishes to engulf us, can;
Soft is the muscle, soft the man.

Of such I ask, . . . (but they have eyes
For ears; everybody stares, nobody hears)
"Were it not wise
To wear in winter warmer clothing?"
For such I feel—for I am busy and have no time to hate
　　—an absent-minded loathing.

"NOËL! NOËL!"

(Reflections before Christmas, 1940)

Nothing will be done. Nothing, nothing at all.
Too bad, poor boy, to have died that cruel death
In vain, Jesus, my dear.

Who loves you now?—I can think of one or two
Who learned to be kind, reading what was written of
    you,
You, incredibly—for it is rare among the young—kind;
This, this enchanted the mind.
You were severe, as well, that's true.
The young are still severe, this year's commencement
    crop's
Extremely so, most arrogant and severe.
They argue with their elders, as you used to do.
There the resemblance stops.

But you, you were charming: we fell in love with you.

One of us still is kind, kind the four seasons through.
You would have loved and scorned him, for he has no
    plan,
He has only pity, he is foolish with pity, a soft man.

[36]

Some of us still, on your birthday, and on the day when
	girls
Walking with their mothers wear violets down Fifth
	Avenue
(Orchids or gardenias preferred—but what can you do,
If your uncle with a bad knee sends them?)
And turn with gentle smiles, almost with leisure
Their bright spring hats and artificial curls this way and
	that,
Saying, with no irritation, almost with good manners, as
	if it were a pleasure
To be walking even with one's mother, on Easter Day
"Shall we walk home this way?"

Some of us still—for ours was an early passion
And hot, and did not last—
Recalling with the aid of the calendar the past,
Suddenly send you roses (*Charitable Deeds*); not any
For months, and then too many;
In fleeting penance for a long and sweet transgression.

Nothing will be done. Oh, nothing. Nothing at all.
The treasure-filled city will fall;
The porcelain vase crumple in the coarse hand, much to
	the general amusement, and blood from minor cuts
	be sticky on the exquisite shards.

For the young, who have not known you, disown you
with loud and solemn talk;
And the old think only of what we once called gold; a
symbol still of greed,
Clutching with arthritic fingers all that they have, much
more than they need,
While with feet disgustingly agile for feet that cannot
walk
They push into piles more property, more power . . .
and not a hand retards
The wheezing clock, which even now groans towards the
loud hour.

Sad, sad, poor boy, to have died that awful death for such
a shifty brood.
Candidates for office, if they're shrewd, say grace before
food,
As they drink only water at the table;
They also go to church, and hearing of the brotherhood
Of man, reflect a while, like Cain, on Abel.

Few speak the truth. Nobody expects them to.
And few have courage. And as for paying any attention
to you,
In a civilized world like ours, what you said, why it just
sounds funny—
About loving your neighbour as yourself, I mean, and
giving away your cloak.

[38]

Well, you *couldn't* take it seriously, you must see that for
    yourself; though one daren't make a joke
About it, because This Government's got Ideals! . . .
And it's pretty touchy about them; you can understand
    the way it feels.

No, you mustn't make jokes about the Bible—oh, it's not
    just you,
It's that crafty old Jacob, taking candy from babies, and
    that lying old Saul,
And that psalm-singing murderous old wife-stealer David,
    and that celibate St. Paul
With about as much charity as a weasel, *they're* sacred,
    too.

So every Sunday, particularly if it's a pleasant day,
Looking saintly (some like beautiful coloured glass, others
    exquisitely carved and stony)
The Tinkling Cymbals, with their minds on their ali-
    mony,
And the Sounding Brass, with its stripes still running the
    right way,
Are photographed walking to church,—oh, the whole
    thing's phony.

But I tell you—lest you weep in earnest, for a whole
world weep—
Who wept but once, and for a friend, in the records that
we hold
(So few, so dearer than gold, yea, than much fine gold)
That there are some, that there are one or two, who truly
love you, and who try to keep—
Who truly try, bad swimmers all (and the beach not
near)—
To keep afloat, not drown, yet at the same time hold aloft
and out of reach
Of the slapping waves, safe from the sea's harm,
With trembling arm your heavy Commandment . . .
even when Sleep
To the despairing mind wears a kinder look than you do
and one is glad the sea is deep; those few
Whose brief instructions clear from the hazy mind upon
the pounding ear are: *you*
Never to jettison.

I wanted to tell you about us, how wicked we are.
And yet also to say that the Star—you know the star I
mean—
Is for some of us clearly visible still in the east at mid-
night rising, and all the night long burns serene—
And that on such nights on unaccustomed knees we
kneel and in sweet discomfort
Pray for hours, and mean it, to be better than we are.

I am not one of these, I fear;
I loved you always for the things I read
About you in a book we had.
I did not meet you for the first time through the incense
and stale smell
Of a room seldom aired, where people purred of heaven
and howled of hell.
I used to read all day, when I was ten:
—You and Don Quijote were my heroes then.

Perhaps because of him I have been kind
Often with my heart, before consulting my mind.
I might have been wiser, had I learned direct from you—
Learned to make curlicues in the sand or on a scratch-pad
while deciding what to say or do . . .
Such as, "Sin—the waves come in—all pushing pebbles
—each alone . . .
I have it!—Let him among them who is *without sin!*—
cast the first stone!"

I learned so young to know you, I could never see
Why we should not be playmates; you were wonderful,—
Oh, you were shiny!—and for some strange reason, fond
of me.

But nothing will be done. I can do nothing. Nothing at
    all.
Only remember what you said, your voice, the way you
    said it,—
For it never was like something read, it was something
    heard, even while I read it—
And try to be wiser and kinder, in a world where Pity
    from place to place
Flees under cover of darkness, hiding her face;
Give Pity breathing-space.

IV

THE CROOKÈD CROSS

A PLAY IN ONE ACT, DONE AFTER THE MANNER OF THE
MEDIAEVAL SACRED MYSTERY PLAYS

(Scene: A room in a Convent School on the out-
skirts of Paris. Twelve little girls are being taught
to do fine sewing under the direction of Sister
Sainte Hélène)

ROSALIE

Oh, tell me, Sister Sainte Hélène,—
That Crookèd Cross,—what can it be,
I saw reflected in the Seine?

SISTER STE. HÉLÈNE
(*in a strained voice*)

Hush, hush, Rosalie.
You did not see—it was a dream—
That flag reflected in the stream.

ROSALIE

But, Sister dear, Theresa, too,
Saw it!—

CATHERINE

And so did I—Did you,
Cecilia?

CECILIA

Yes, I did. But I
Saw it above me in the sky,—
Like a black spider—oh, it seemed—

SISTER STE. HÉLÈNE

Child! Child! This is a dream you dreamed!

CECILIA

No, Sister, no! I *saw* it there!—
A Crookèd Cross in the bright air,
As black as Evil, Sister!—oh,
'Twas wicked that it should be so,
On *Notre Dame*!

SISTER STE. HÉLÈNE
(*with a stifled cry*)
Ah!
    (*pause, then with great self-control, quietly*)
That will do,
Cecilia. Children, go about
Your work . . . These stitches must come out—
Yes, back to here, Theresa. See
How coarse they look?—Give that to me
A moment, Catherine.

CATHERINE

I don't know
Just how the *corner* ought to go,
Sister.

[46]

SISTER STE. HÉLÈNE
(*as if to herself*)

Can *not*—can *not*—be so.

CATHERINE
(*timidly, after a pause*)

Sister—

SISTER STE. HÉLÈNE
(*recollecting herself, briskly and in a*
would-be matter-of-fact voice)

That is not hard to do.
Cecilia, you have trouble, too,
I think, with this part.—First you *fold*,
You see—

CATHERINE
(*doubtfully*)

Yes.—Sister, are *you cold?*
Your hand is shaking dreadfully!

SISTER STE. HÉLÈNE
(*almost harshly*)

'Tis nothing.
            (*sternly to a young girl who has just*
            entered, with her arms full of roses,
            out of breath and excited)
You are *late*, Marie.
Twice late—I think—within a *week*.

[47]

(in a whisper to Cecilia)

Goodness, I never heard her speak
So crossly—biting off your head
For the least *thing*—

CECILIA
(to Catherine, whispering)

It's just a *shame!*

MARIE

Oh, Sister! I am not to blame!
Truly I'm not! Forgive me, *please*—
My mother said to bring you these—
"Cut *all* of them, I might as well,"
She said—
                    *(pause, as if puzzled and
                    wondering, then happily)*
Oh, Sister, don't they smell
Sweet?—It takes a long time, though,
        (as if trying to explain her tardiness)
To cut so many roses—Oh,
I do love roses—*(regretfully)* they're the last
We'll have, she said—I don't see *why!*
They *always* bloom all through July—
And *June* is not quite half way past—
Well, anyway, *(sighing)* they'll be the last,
My mother said.—*(eagerly)* I'll care for them
Each morning, Sister, if I may.

[48]

I think if I cut every stem
And change the water every day,—
They'll last much longer in that way.

> SISTER STE. HÉLÈNE
> *(drily)*

Doubtless. But you can scarcely be
Late every morning, then, Marie.
> *(there is an astonished silence)*

> MARIE
> *(quaveringly)*

Why, Sister—I—*(bursts into sobs)*

> CATHERINE
> *(whispering to Cecilia)*

She's being *mean*!
She really is!—I've never *seen*—

> CECILIA
> *(whispering to Catherine)*

She hasn't even *thanked* her yet—
And all those roses!—

> SISTER STE. HÉLÈNE
> *(in a strained voice)*

I regret—
Dear child—come here.—Oh, if my arm
Might shield you *always* from black harm
And heavy grief! alas!—alas!

(almost wildly)

Must I behold your bright days pass
Into *that shadow?*—*(quietly)* Please forget
My words. I am—distraught—upset,
I fear.—

MARIE
*(in an awed voice, as if she were
telling of having seen a ghost)*

Oh, Sister!—So am I!
I saw a *Black Flag* in the sky!—
A Crookèd Cross—I'd seen, somewhere,—
In pictures, maybe, but not—*there!*
It did not move! There was a breeze—
The leaves of the horse chestnut trees
Were moving; and the lime trees, too!
It did not float as our flags do
So prettily, red, white and blue;
Or flap, or tug, or whip about
The standard,—no, it stood straight out
As if 'twere made of something—oh,
Metal!—It frightened me, you know;
For all the flags I'd ever seen
Were made of—*you* know what I mean—

CECILIA

Of serge, or silk!

[50]

MARIE

Yes, anyway,
Stuff that is strong, I mean to say,
Yet is not hard!

CECILIA

Stuff you could hold
Against your cheek, and not feel cold!
Nor fear that it might bruise your skin—

MARIE

Stuff you could wrap a baby in!

CECILIA

This flag (*the one I saw today*)
And feared, and hated, right away,—
A Crookèd Cross, and black as ink—
Was made of iron, I truly think.

SISTER STE. HÉLÈNE
(*quietly, but as if somewhat mad*)

Cecilia, there could never be
An iron flag. You did not see
The thing you speak of. You,—you, too,
You dreamed this; dreamed it, all of you.

CECILIA

But, Sister, something deep inside—
For it *was there*, so black, so strong,

[51]

Where, *surely*, it did not belong . . .
I shook my fist at it; I cried
"What will the Blessed Virgin do,
You ugly thing, when she sees you?
Up there, in sight of all the town,
On *Notre Dame?*—She'll tear you down!—
As soon as ever the Baby wakes
To die again for all our sakes,
Who's sleeping now on Holy Knee—
When He wakes up, you'll see! You'll see!"

SISTER STE. HÉLÈNE
(with terrible intensity)

Cecilia, look me in the face.
You-did-not-see-in-such-a-place
The—look at me—the thing you seemed
To see. Cecilia, you-have-dreamed.

CECILIA
(pause)

Yes, Sister.—*(passionately)* Oh, it can't be true
You think that I have lied to you!
And how could *anybody* make
Me dream when I was wide awake?
And, Sister, there was something more!
I turned and tried the little door
To Mary's House—I wished to weep,
(Unless the Child were still asleep)

[52]

On Mary's heart—and in her ear
Whisper the thing she'd *have* to hear
Sooner or later . . . I was shocked
To find the little door was locked!
Why, Sister! Sister Sainte Hélène!
What is it? Speak! Are you in pain?
Oh, run, Theresa! Anne! Lucie!
Bring help!

> (*Enter Mother Superior*)

Oh, Mother Rose-Marie,
What have I done?—What have I said?
She lies so still—she is not dead,
Is she?—

> (*the little girls begin to sob
> softly—or say, "Oh—Oh—"*)

MOTHER SUPERIOR

Hush . . . hush. She's trying to speak.
Lean closer—

SISTER STE. HÉLÈNE
(*in a low weak voice*)

Dream . . .

> (*pause*)

CECILIA

> (*whispering to Catherine*)

She sounds so *weak*!

[53]

CATHERINE
(whispering to Cecilia)

Oh!—I'm afraid!

ROSALIE
(suddenly and in a frightened voice)

She said "Extreme,"
Mother . . . *(she sobs)*
(the children gasp, in awe and sorrow)

MOTHER SUPERIOR

No. No.—The word was "Dream" . . .
*(children cry "Oh! Oh!" and weep heart-brokenly;
then stop as the Mother Superior speaks again)*
She said that . . . something . . . is . . . a
dream.
(the children weep softly)

CURTAIN

V

SONNETS

I

PEACE was my earliest love, and I presume
Will be my latest; but today, adult,
Arguing not to prove but for result
Opposing concepts in this thoughtful room,
I wonder at whose prompting, schooled by whom
I urged that Peace the Slogan, Peace the Cult,
Could turn the edge of sledge and catapult
And leave us calm to cull the grafted bloom.

In all my life I never knew a thing
So highly prized to be so cheaply had:
Longing to wed with Peace, what did we do?—
Sketched her a fortress on a paper pad;
Under her casement twanged a lovesick string;
Left wide the gate that let her foemen through.

II

"GENTLEMEN CRY, PEACE!"

THERE is no Peace; had we again the choice
Whether to build our sinews to such force
None dare affront us, or to seek divorce
From the blunt, factual time, and with soft voice
Blandish the past to give us back our toys
Faded but still so dear,—we should of course
Forego tranquillity without remorse,
Gird us for battle . . . and in peace rejoice.

But now . . . what power to bargain have the poor?
And, in those iron values which alone
Pass in our time for legal currency,
Minted by savage chieftains to insure
Shut mouth, shut mind, hushed sobbing, swallowed groan
And punished laughter—who so poor as we?

III

WHILE London, while Berlin—two cities dear
To those who live in them—burn to the ground,
Our statesmen fiddle on, a twiddling sound
Most unmelodious to a well-tuned ear:
Of two corrupt machines which shall appear,
Grinning, on balconies with bunting bound,
Victorious in November?—theme profound!
So turns toward death the sad, ignoble year.

To what vulgarities, to what abyss
Of cheap dishonour clownish and obscene,
Have you not sunk, O my belovèd land?
What sacrifice Herculean out of this
Can lift you up?—and sweep these stables clean?
Ask it, America! Demand! Demand!

IV

Only the ruthless, now, so it would seem,
Have courage and risk all; reluctant, slow,
Afraid of what's to come and where's to go,
Defense crawls feebly, like a half-dried stream
Past boulders, towards a town whose drought's extreme—
So it would seem, I say; it is not so:
We are so sound asleep, how can we know
What thirst and want surround our sunny dream?

Men wide-awake, men well-equipped, well-fed
On certainty, attack the slumbering towns;
Blood was their breakfast, conquest is their goal:
But men asleep can stumble out of bed
And pull their trousers on, and find their guns,
And fight, to save from rape the human soul.

V

You find "outrageous" this?—these outraged hearts?—
Homes, griefs invaded?—customs, pious praise
Denied?—these hungry peasants forced to raise
Loved roots for hated conquerors? Counterparts
Of all such evil deeds, red on the charts
Of earlier wars, though done in earlier ways,
Track us like drops of blood down all our days;
One difference note: *Noblesse Oblige* departs.
It is the fashion now for kings to flee,
Captains betray; who stands behind his guns?
Some simple man, with no great gifts endowed.
Oh, rich and terrible times!—when we may see,
Between the moon's mild rising and the sun's,
Kings sprint for cover, and their slaves too proud.

VI

I MUST not die of pity; I must live;
Grow strong, not sicken; eat, digest my food,
That it may build me, and in doing good
To blood and bone, broaden the sensitive
Fastidious pale perception: we contrive
Lean comfort for the starving, who intrude
Upon them with our pots of pity: brewed
From stronger meat must be the broth we give.

Blue, bright September day, with here and there
On the green hills a maple turning red,
And white clouds racing in the windy air!—
If I would help the weak, I must be fed
In wit and purpose, pour away despair
And rinse the cup, eat happiness like bread.

VII

CHAFE with your maiden breasts, O Shunammite,
The chilly feet anointed and unclean
Of David, lest cold Death should come between,
And an old man lie quiet in the night;
Peer once again, Alcestis, down the flight
Of steps that drop to Hades; let him screen
His eyes, your ransomed spouse; who yet has seen
His agèd parents buy him life and light?

Only the young, who had so much to give,
Gave France their all; the old, whose valorous past
(In anecdote not only: in bronze cast)
Might teach a frightened courage how to live,
Wheedled by knaves, from action fugitive,
Sold their son's hopes, to make their porridge last.

VIII

Where does he walk, or sit and stir his tea,
Or rise to speak, this moment, who will give
When the day comes (*that the Conservative*
Party retain its prominence, and he
And a few friends their ancient property,
Trout-stream and shooting-box, and chance to live
A few more gouty winters) who will give,
When the day comes, England to Germany?

Somewhere he breathes; and would his breath might stop
Before he does the deed he has in mind;
Old men grow feeble, but do traitors drop
Ever, before the ugly note is signed?
I know of no such instance: greed would prop
The pen, though the dead arm relaxed behind.

IX

How innocent of me and my dark pain
In the clear east, unclouded save for one
Flamingo-coloured feather, combed and spun
Into fine spirals, with ephemeral stain
To dye the morning rose after the rain,
Rises the simple and majestic sun,
His azure course, well-known and often-run
With patient brightness to pursue again.

The gods are patient: they are slaves of Time
No less than we, and longer, at whose call
Must Phoebus rise and mount his dewy car,
And lift the reins and start the ancient climb;
Could we learn patience, though day-creatures all,
Our day should see us godlier than we are.

Set in Linotype Fairfield
Format by A. W. Rushmore
Manufactured by the Haddon Craftsmen
for the publishers HARPER & BROTHERS
New York and London